6|14

D1242590

6|14

This library edition published in 2014 by Walter Foster Publishing,
a Division of the Quayside Publishing Group.
Walter Foster Library
3 Wrigley, Suite A
Irvine, CA 92618

U.S. publication copyright © 2013 Walter Foster Publishing. International copyright reserved
in all countries. No part of this book may be reproduced in any form without written permis-
sion from the publisher.
All rights reserved. Walter Foster is a registered trademark.

Distributed in the United States and Canada by
Lerner Publisher Services
241 First Avenue North
Minneapolis, MN 55401 U.S.A.
www.lernerbooks.com

First Library Edition

Library of Congress Cataloging-in-Publication Data

Cuddy, Robbin, author, illustrator.
  All about farm & forest animals / step-by-step illustrations by Robbin Cuddy. -- Library edition.
    pages cm
  "Learn to draw more than 40 barnyard animals and wildlife critters step by step."
  ISBN 978-1-93958-110-5
  1. Animals in art--Juvenile literature. 2. Drawing--Technique--Juvenile literature. I. Title. II. Title:
All about farm and forest animals.
  NC780.C83 2014
  743.6--dc23
                                                                              2013024998

012014
18376

9 8 7 6 5 4 3 2 1

All About
DRAWING

Farm & Forest Animals

Step-by-step illustrations by Robbin Cuddy

DR CASS COUNTY PUBLIC LIBRARY
400 E. MECHANIC
HARRISONVILLE, MO 64701

0 0022 0437974 3

Table of Contents

Getting Started

When you **look** closely at the **drawings** in this book, you'll notice that they're made up of basic shapes, such as circles, triangles, and rectangles. To draw all your favorite animal friends, just start with simple shapes as you see here. It's easy and fun!

Circles are used to draw heads, chests, and hips.

Ovals

make good profile heads and bodies.

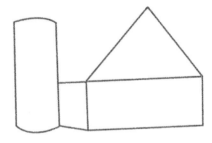

Triangles

are best for angled parts, like the roof of a barn.

FIND THE SHAPE!

Can you find circles, ovals, and triangles on these animals? Look closely at the raccoon's head and body, and then check out the rabbit's oval-shaped ears. It's easy to see the basic shapes in any animal once you know what to look for!

Drawing Exercises

Warm up your hand by drawing lots of squiggles and shapes.

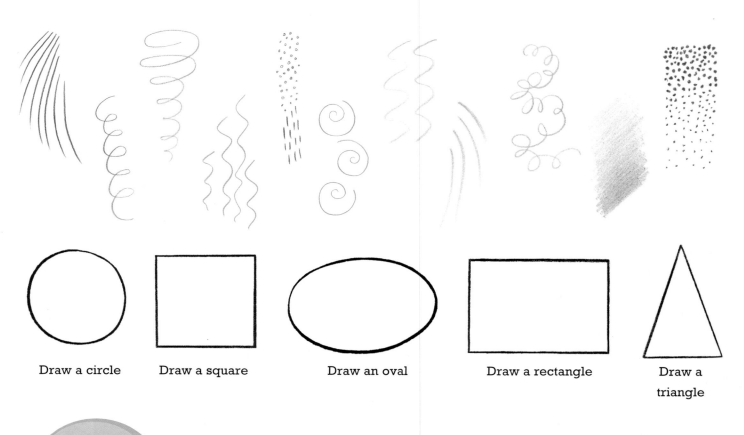

Draw a circle   Draw a square   Draw an oval   Draw a rectangle   Draw a triangle

FUN TIP!

With an assortment of animals to portray, the color possibilities are endless! Before you pick a coloring tool for your drawing, think about the animal's different textures. Is its skin furry, feathered, scaled, or smooth? Colored pencils have a sharp tip that is great for tiny details like small hairs and feathers. Crayons can be used to cover large areas quickly and markers make your colors appear more solid. Or try watercolor for a soft touch.

Tools & Materials

Gather some drawing tools, such as paper, a pencil, an eraser, and a pencil sharpener. When you're finished drawing you can add color with crayons, colored pencils, markers, or even paint.

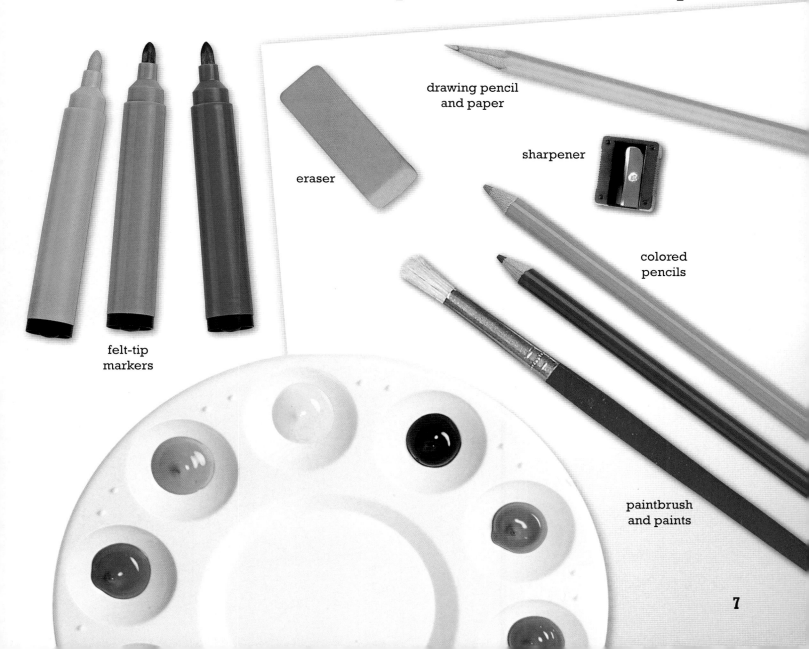

drawing pencil
and paper

sharpener

eraser

colored
pencils

felt-tip
markers

paintbrush
and paints

Grizzly Bear

The **large** brown bear has a **hump** on its shoulders. It got the name "grizzly," meaning "gray-haired," for its white-tipped fur.

5

AT RISK

Grizzlies used to be common in North America, but are now *endangered,* or in danger of dying off. Only 1,000 to 1,400 remain in the United States because of illegal hunting, man-made buildings and roads, and loss of natural food sources.

6

FUN FACT

Grizzly bears hibernate for four to six months!

Cow

One of the **largest** animals on the **farm,** dairy cows produce milk. The most common dairy cow has a black-and-white pattern on its body. Others are brown and white, all brown, or all black.

5

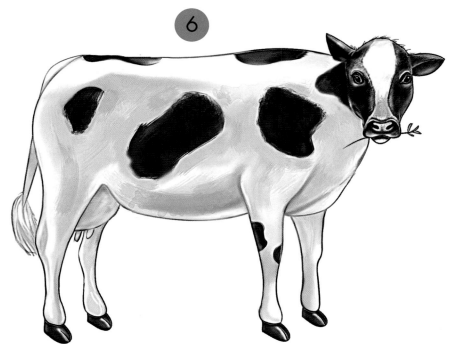

6

FUN FACT

A dairy cow's milk goes further than the breakfast table. It is used to create a variety of products, such as cheese, butter, yogurt, and ice cream!

Wolf

The wolf is the **largest** member of the **dog** family. Wolves range in color from snowy white to gray, reddish-brown, and all black.

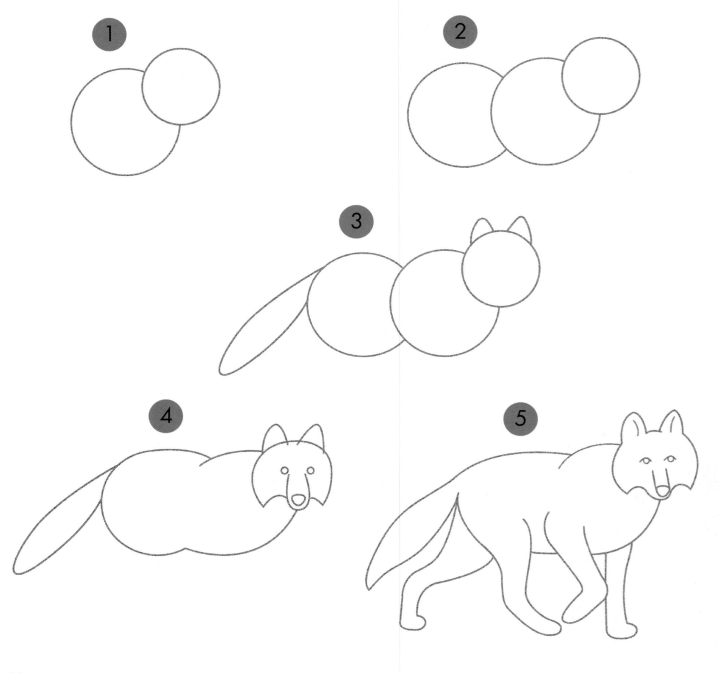

Wolves almost became *extinct,* or died out, in North America. But their numbers are growing because they have been moved to protected lands.

6

7

Young wolf pups love to play. They play hide-and-seek, catch, tag, and wrestling games. Playing helps them learn how to hunt and get along with other wolves.

Moose

Male moose are known for their **huge antlers**, which can grow up to six feet across. Moose have humped shoulders and long faces. A "bell," or flap of skin, hangs from their necks.

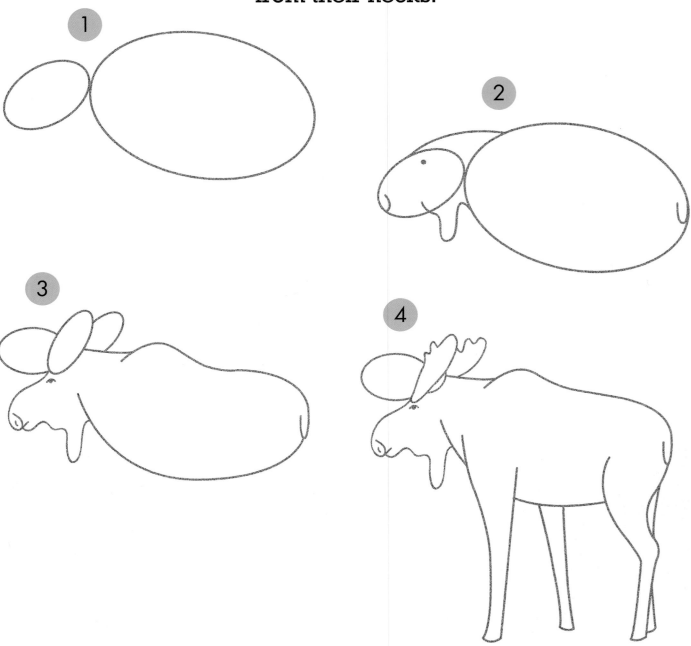

5

6

FUN FACT

Moose have four separate areas in their stomachs. They *ruminate,* or re-chew, food that comes back up from the front part of the stomach. A moose stomach can hold up to 100 pounds of food!

Sheep

Sheep have a thick **coat** used to create **wool** for blankets and other items. Farmers shave their sheep's fleece in the spring. The sheep have the rest of the year to grow their fluffy coats back.

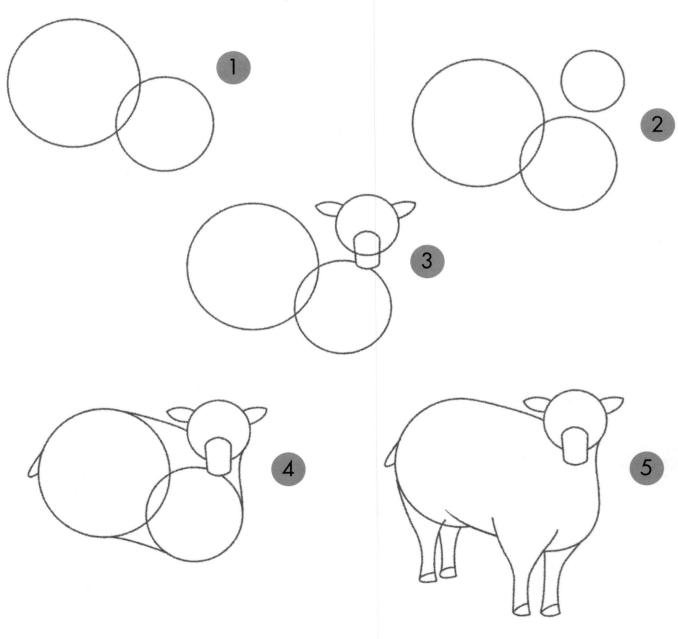

6

7

FUN FACT

A sheep's wool is naturally fire-resistant. Wool is difficult to ignite because it needs extreme heat in order to burn. Because of this, wool is often used to make household carpets safer.

Bull

An adult male **cow** is called a bull. The **large**, powerful bull has a wide head, two large horns, and a broad chest. Bulls are also more muscular than female cows.

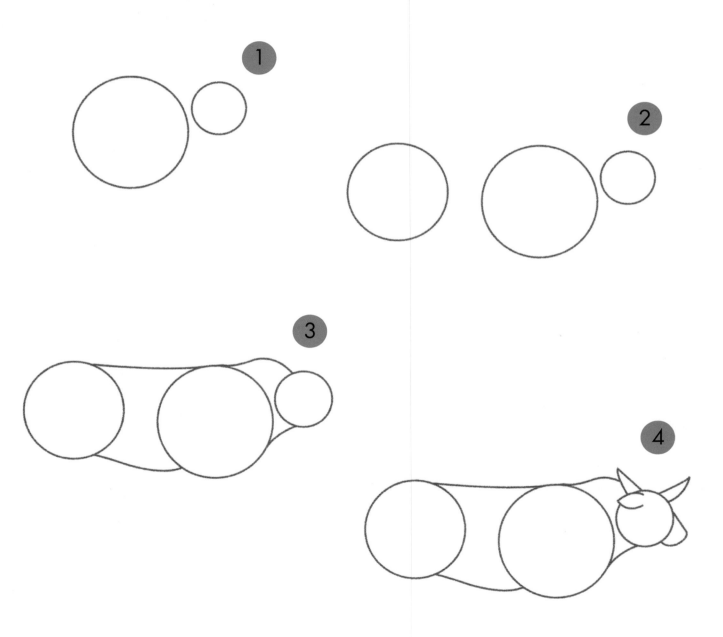

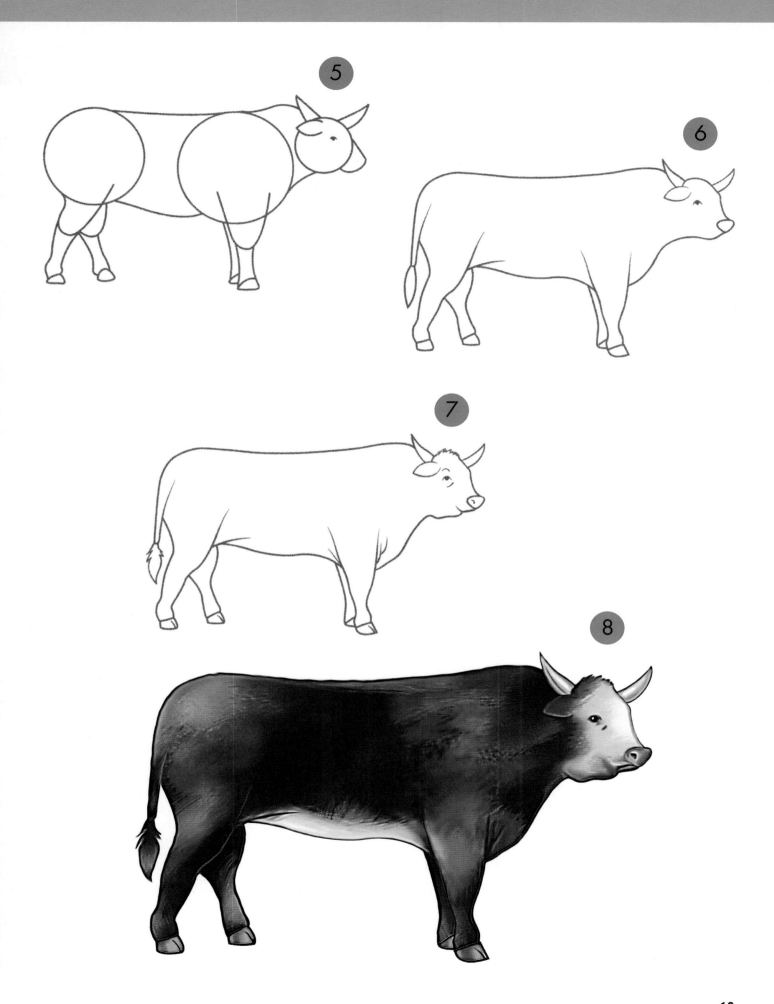

Pig

Pink skin, a flat broad snout, and a **curly** tail are a few traits of the lovable pig. Pigs have small eyes and poor vision, so they use their snout to help them smell their surroundings.

5

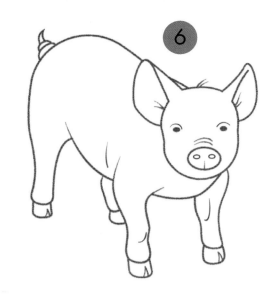

6

7

FUN FACT

Pigs don't sweat! To keep them cool in the summer, some farmers use sprinklers to mist them with water. Pigs will also roll around in mud to stay cool!

Bison

Bison, also called **buffalo**, have shaggy brown **fur** and a large hump on their shoulders. They are known for their long beards and two curved horns.

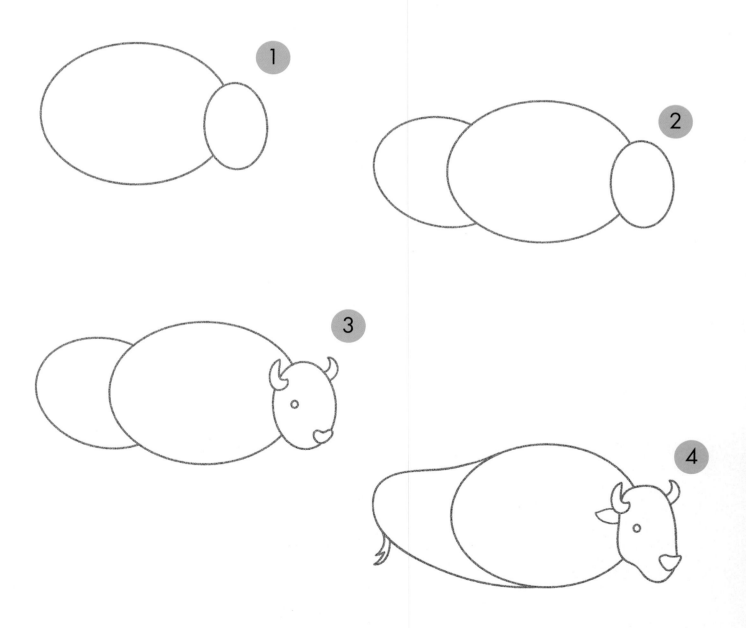

5

6

7

FUN FACT

The American bison's ancestor is the prehistoric long-horned bison. It crossed a land bridge from Asia to North America during the Ice Age with other giant mammals. Millions of bison roamed the Great Plains before hunters killed many of them during the 19th century. Today only bison with short horns exist, and they are protected by the government.

23

Antelope

Antelope are a group of animals with **horns** and **hooves**.
Their horns can be long, short, curved, branched,
or even twisted spirals!

5

6

FUN FACT

You may think that antelope are related to deer; however, they are part of an animal family that includes cattle, goats, and sheep. Deer shed their antlers every year, but antelope keep their horns for life.

Rocky Mountain Goat

Rocky Mountain goats have a long **beard** and two **horns** that curve backward. Their thick, white fur keeps them warm and helps them blend into the snow.

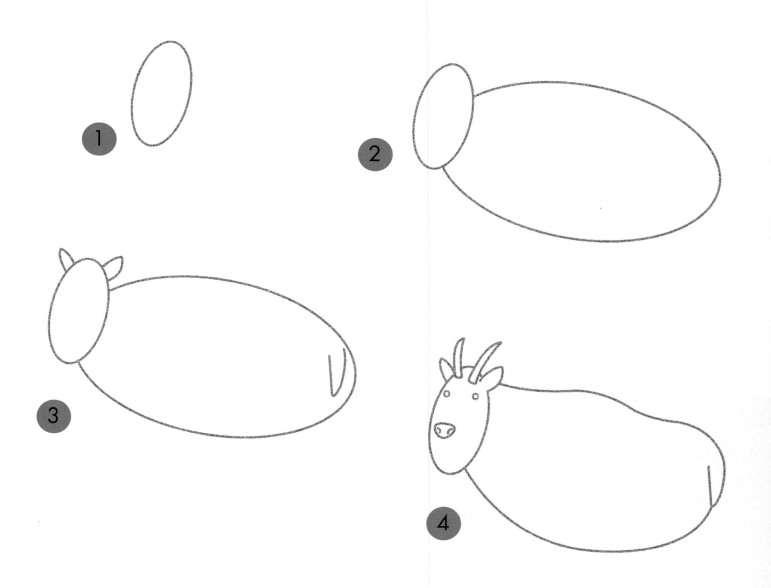

5

6

7

FUN FACT

Rocky Mountain goats can climb icy, rocky cliffs and leap from rock to rock. Their hooves have two toes and rough pads for balance and grip. Few animals—or humans—can reach the Rocky Mountain goat's home high up in the snowy peaks.

Stag Deer

Male red deer, or **stags**, have **antlers**.
Their antlers are branched with long, hard pointy ends.

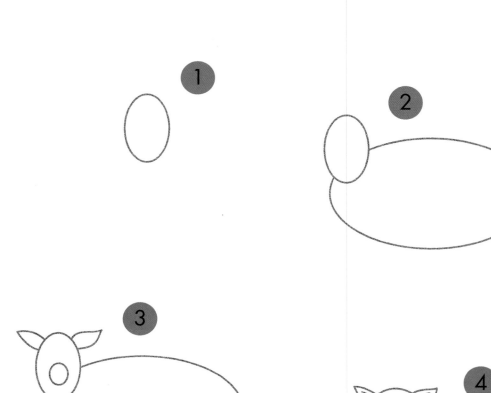

5

6

7

FUN FACT

Stags have roaring contests and walk side by side to see which one is bigger and stronger. Sometimes fights break out, but usually the larger stag with the louder voice wins without even touching his rival.

Goat

Farmers generally keep goats for their **milk**. Goats are known for having long beards. Female goats are called **does**, and male goats are called **bucks**.

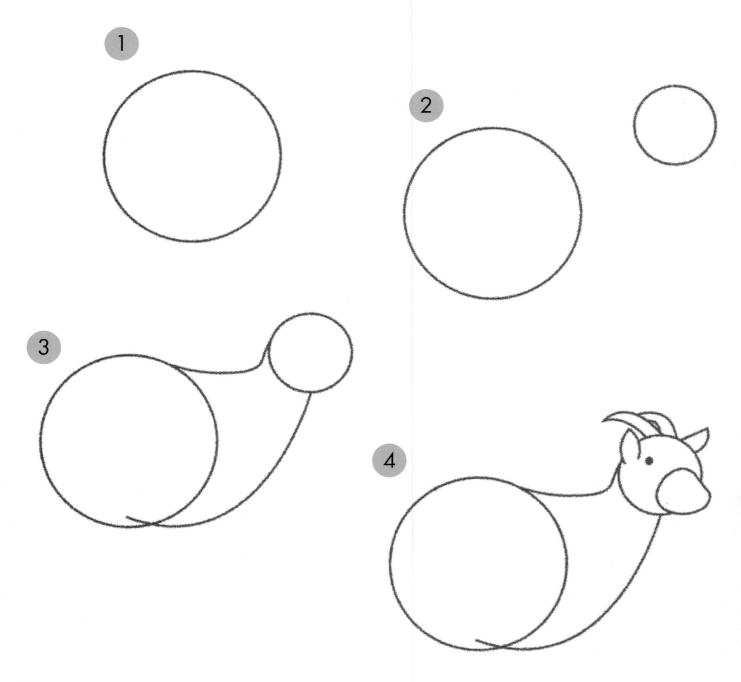

Turkey

Turkeys have **wide**, squat bodies and **short** beaks. Male turkeys have long, red wattles below their beaks and down their necks. A turkey will raise its tail and fan its feathers to appear larger and more powerful.

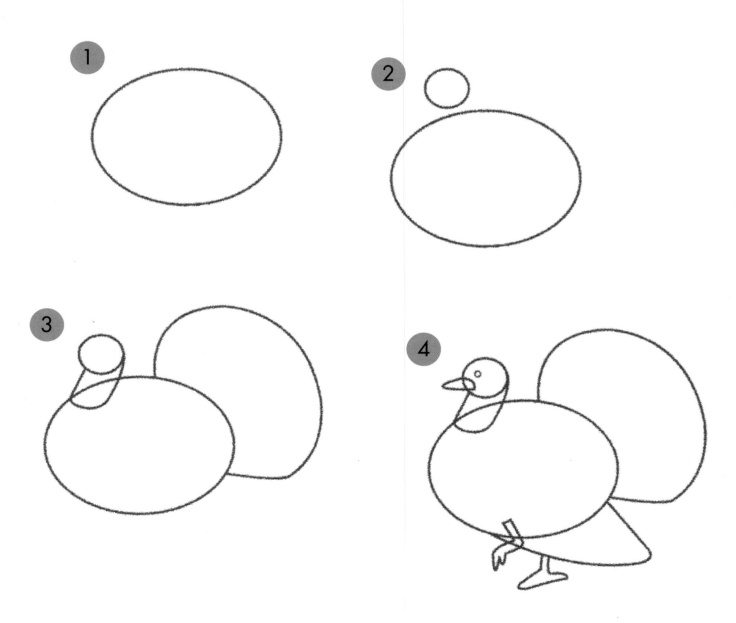

FUN FACT

Female turkeys are not as colorful as the larger, showy males. Most females have brown feathers with some white, light stripes. Males have vivid tail feathers—which are often black and amber with spots of gold and green—to intimidate other male turkeys.

Duck

This **waterfowl** lives on the farm's pond or stream. A duck's **webbed** feet act like little underwater paddles, making it an excellent swimmer and causing it to waddle when it walks.

FUN FACT

Ducks have special feathers that are covered in a layer of oil, making them waterproof. The soft inner feathers stay dry, keeping the ducks nice and warm.

Duckling

Ducklings **spend** the first few weeks of **life** following their mother's every move. This is how they learn where to find food, where to swim, and how long to swim before their feathers absorb too much water.

FUN FACT

Ducklings are usually born in the spring through early summer. That's because female ducks lay more eggs when the daylight is longer.

Donkey

Donkeys **look** similar to **horses**, but they are usually smaller with shorter, stockier legs, and longer, wider ears. In some countries, donkeys are used to pull carts and plow fields.

Bald Eagle

The bald eagle has a white head and tail. Instead of flapping its wings, the bald eagle soars through the sky with its brown wings extended and nearly flat.

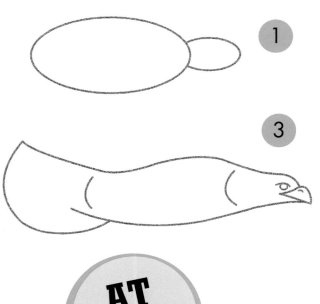

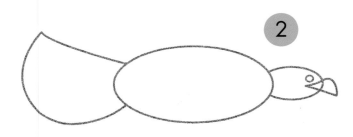

AT RISK

In the mid-1900s, farmers used harmful chemicals called *pesticides* to keep insects from eating their crops. These chemicals leaked into water where bald eagles hunted fish, and the birds became endangered. Fortunately, the government passed laws to control pesticide use, and bald eagle numbers are growing again.

5

6

FUN FACT

The bald eagle is the national bird of the United States. But not all of the founding fathers agreed with this choice—Benjamin Franklin did not want the nation's symbol to be a bird that steals food from other animals. However, he was outvoted and the bald eagle became the U.S. emblem in 1782. It stands for strength and freedom.

Mute Swan

The mute swan has a **snowy white** body and a long, curved neck. It is known for its black face and orange bill.

FUN FACT

Mute swans are not really "mute." They can hiss, snort, and make soft bark-like calls.

Beaver

Beavers have large front **teeth**, a flat **tail**, and webbed feet. They tend to be a bit clumsy on land, but they are very graceful in the water.

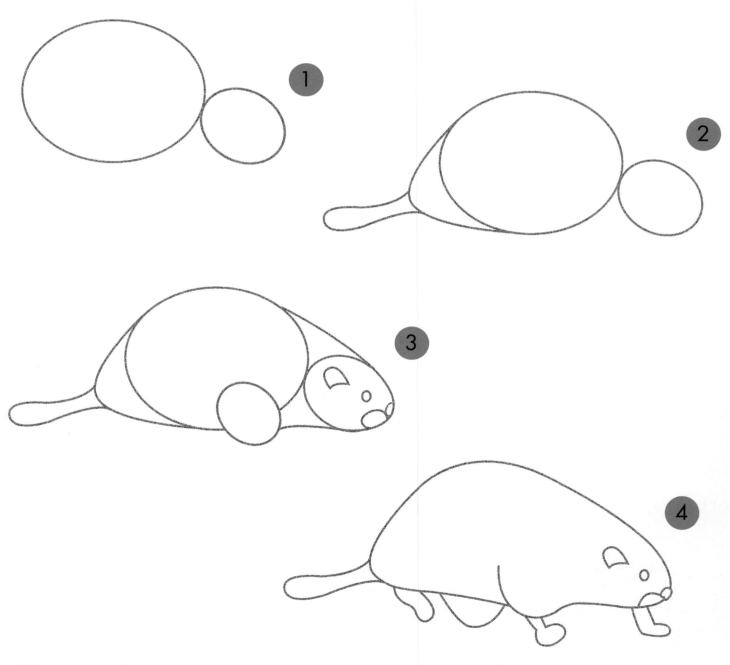

5

6

FUN FACT

Beavers can cut down tall trees with their power-ful teeth and jaws. They build dams to create large ponds. Then they use mud and branches to build dome-like homes, called lodges, in the middle of the pond. Beaver families get in and out of their lodges through secret, underwater entrances.

Bobcat

The bobcat is known for its **short** "bobbed" **tail** and spiky ear hair. It also has a mane of fur around its face.

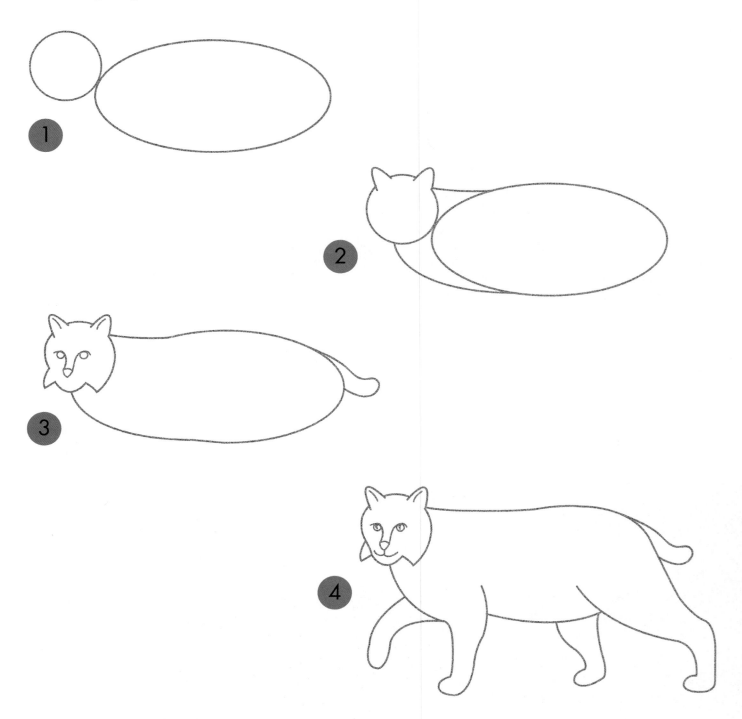

5

6

FUN FACT

Also called wildcats, bobcats are about twice as large as their house-cat relatives. They mew, yowl, hiss, and purr, just like domestic cats, but they are fearless hunters that can pounce on much larger animals.

Border Collie

The Border Collie is the **farmer's loyal** companion. This dog's shaggy fur helps keep it warm in the winter and cool in the summer. Because of its natural instinct to corral a pack, this herding dog helps the farmer drive sheep and cattle.

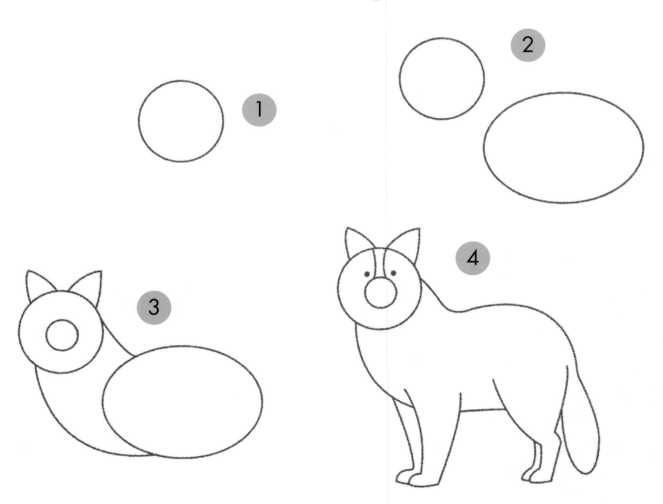

5

6

7

FUN FACT

Border Collies are often referred to as the most intelligent of the dog breeds. They love being active and often perform in agility contests, where they must use their skill and intellect to help them navigate through obstacle courses.

Rooster

The rooster **guards** the hen house. It **sits** high on a perch so it can see intruders and warn hens of impending danger with its distinctive alarm, "cocka-doodle-doo!"

5

FUN FACT

The rooster's distinctive head consists of earlobes; a wattle that hangs from its beak; and a crest, or comb, on the top of its head—all of which are usually bright red.

6

Alpaca

The alpaca is a relative of the **llama** and the **camel**. Farmers raise them for their long, soft fleece, which is used to create supple yarn that can be spun or woven into blankets and clothing.

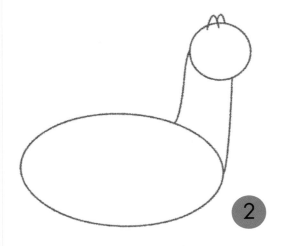

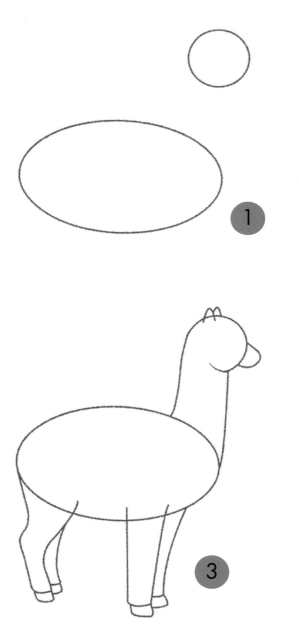

5

6

FUN FACT

Alpaca fleece is prized not only for its soft, silky hair-like quality but also because alpacas come in a variety of shades— more than 50 in all!

51

Goose

On the **farm**, a goose is never alone. Geese **travel** in packs called gaggles, which keep them safe from predators and allow them to fly in a "V" formation during migrations.

Field Mouse

The mouse has large, round **ears** and a long **tail**. Field mice love taking advantage of the loose seeds and food scraps that can be found around the farm and on the barn floor.

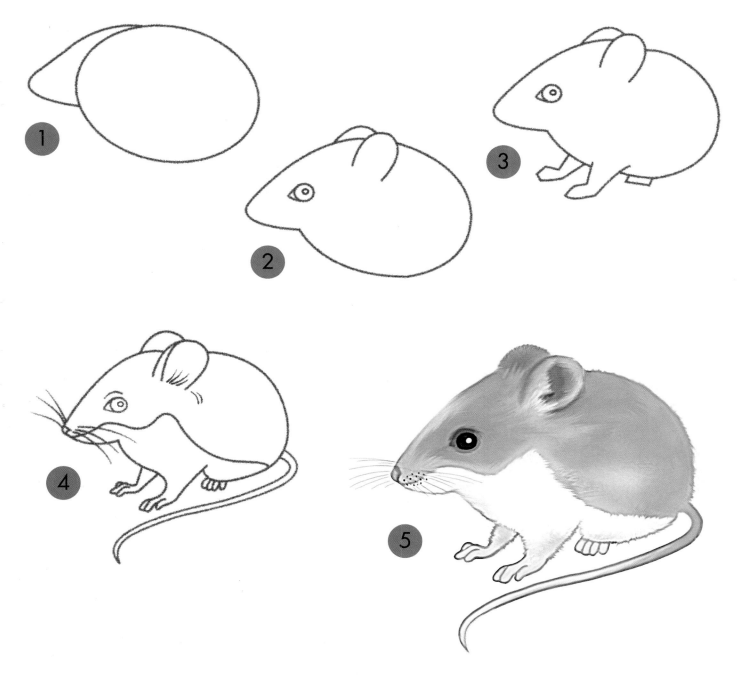

Forest Elephant

Elephants are the largest **mammals** on land.
These gray **giants** flap their huge ears to keep cool.

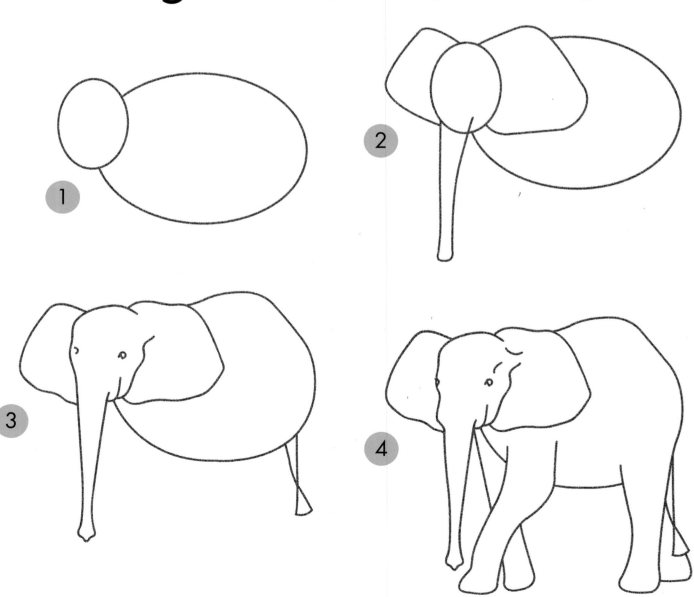

5

6

FUN FACT

An elephant's long trunk has thousands of different muscles used to smell, drink, grab food, and make sounds. It is like a nose, straw, hand, and trumpet all in one!

Mountain Lion

Mountain lions are large **wild** cats with **big** paws and sharp claws. Their back legs are bigger than their front legs, so they can jump high and far.

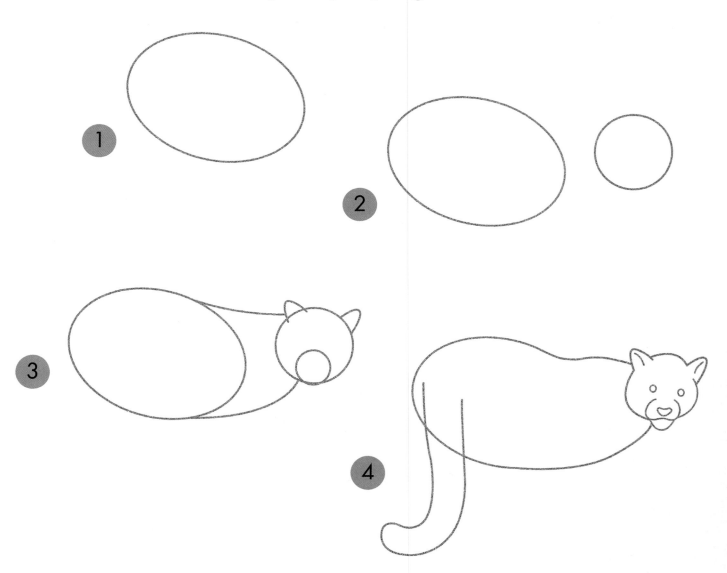

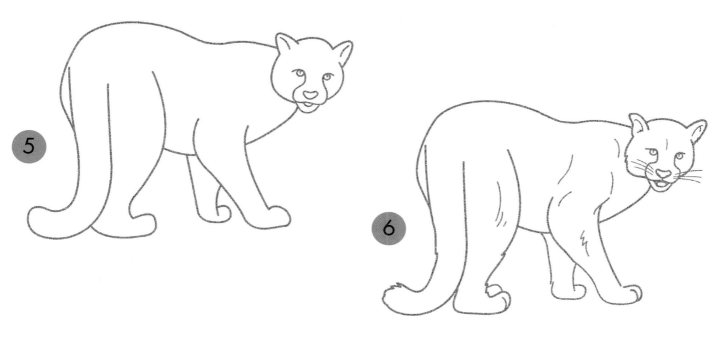

5

6

7

FUN FACT

The term mountain lion is used to identify cats of many breeds, including a puma, cougar, and catamount. The name can also be misleading since these large cats do not live in only mountainous regions and can't actually roar like a lion.

Bighorn Sheep

Male bighorn sheep have large, curved **horns**.
They charge each other with their horns and battle for hours!

5

AT RISK

Some desert bighorn sheep are endangered. The plants and water they need to survive are disappearing because the weather has become hotter and drier where they live.

6

FUN FACT

Baby bighorn sheep are called lambs. They have soft, woolly coats and little horn buds. A one-day-old lamb can keep up with its mother when walking and climbing.

59

Red Fox

The red fox has **orange-red** fur, pointy **black** ears, and a bushy "brush" tail.

FUN FACT

Red foxes are *omnivores*. This means that they eat many different foods, including fruits, plants, and small animals. Red foxes are good hunters. They are smart, have a great sense of smell, and pounce on prey like a cat.

Gray Squirrel

Gray squirrels **spend** most of their time in **trees**. They use their big, bushy tails for balance, shade, warmth, and swimming.

Raccoon

Raccoons are known for the **black mask** around their eyes, as well as their ringed tails. Watch out, or this masked bandit might make off with your food!

1

2

3

4

5

FUN FACT

Raccoons have five fingers on their front feet, so they leave tracks that look like tiny hands. They can do many things, including opening doors, untying knots, or plucking things right out of your pocket!

Chicken

Chickens provide farmers with plenty of **fresh eggs**. Hens love to feed on worms, insects, grains, corn, and other vegetables to give them the energy they need to lay eggs.

Baby Chick

Baby chicks have **soft**, fluffy **feathers** that are not sufficient enough to keep their bodies warm. For the first five weeks of its life, a chick must be kept warm at all times.

FUN FACT

Not all baby chicks are yellow. They are often white, spotted brown, or even black. A chick's feathers will not change color as it ages, so its feathers as a chick will be the color of its feathers as a full-grown chicken!

Coyote

The clever coyote is part of the **dog family.**

It is a great swimmer and a fast runner!

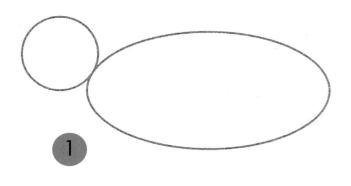

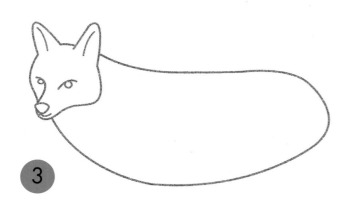

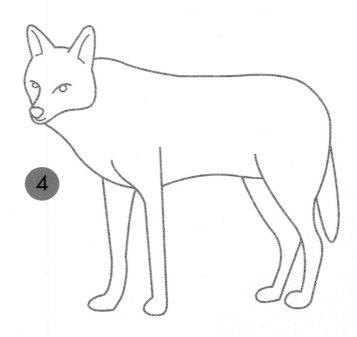

5

6

FUN FACT

Coyotes can be super sneaky and secretive! They often work in pairs or teams to hunt. There are many myths and legends about the coyote that are told to teach lessons about human behavior.

67

Cutthroat Trout

The **spotted** cutthroat trout gets its **name** from the red slash on its throat.

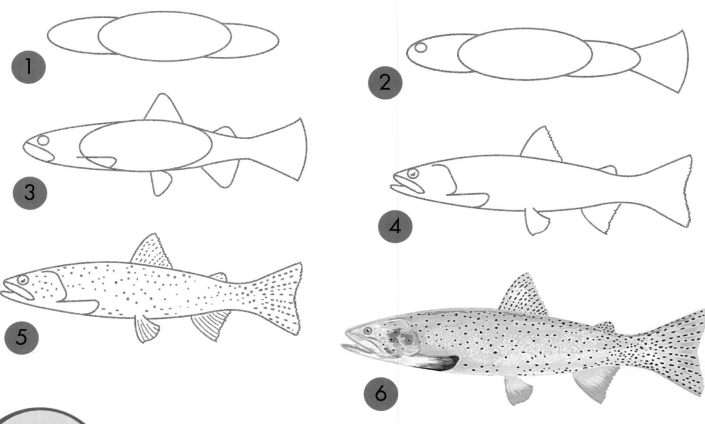

FUN FACT

The cutthroat trout became Wyoming's state fish in 1987. It is the only trout in the state that is *native* to, or originally from, Wyoming.

Prairie Rattlesnake

This snake has a **rattle** on its tail. The **diamond** shapes on its body help it blend in with the ground.

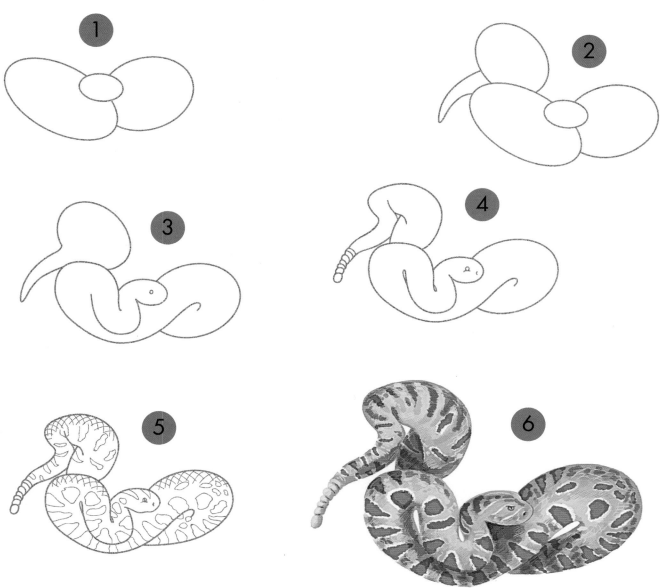

Ostrich

This large, **flightless** bird originated in **Africa**. Some farmers raise ostriches for their eggs and feathers, which are used for decoration. This bird has long, powerful legs and a long neck, which allows it to spot predators.

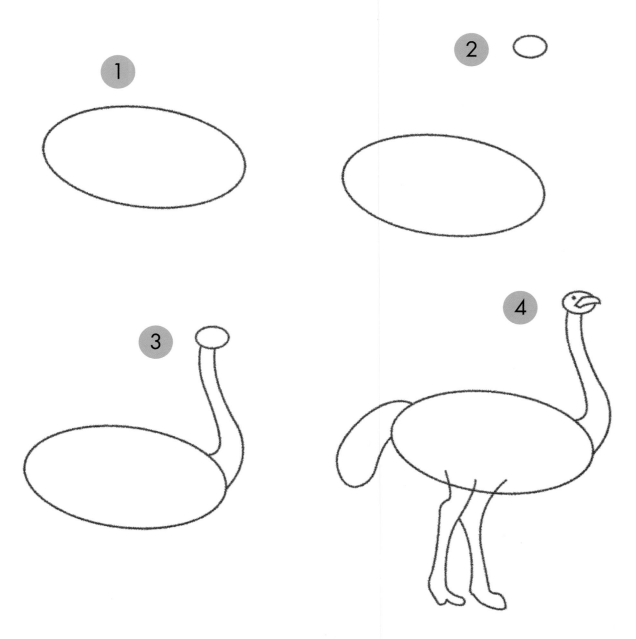

5

6

7

**FUN
FACT**

Male ostriches typically have black feathers
with white ends, while females are solid brown.
Males fan their tails and perform a side-swaying
dance in order to impress and attract females.

Orangutan

Orangutan means "**person** of the **forest**" in Malay. This orange-haired **ape** spends most of its time swinging through forest treetops.

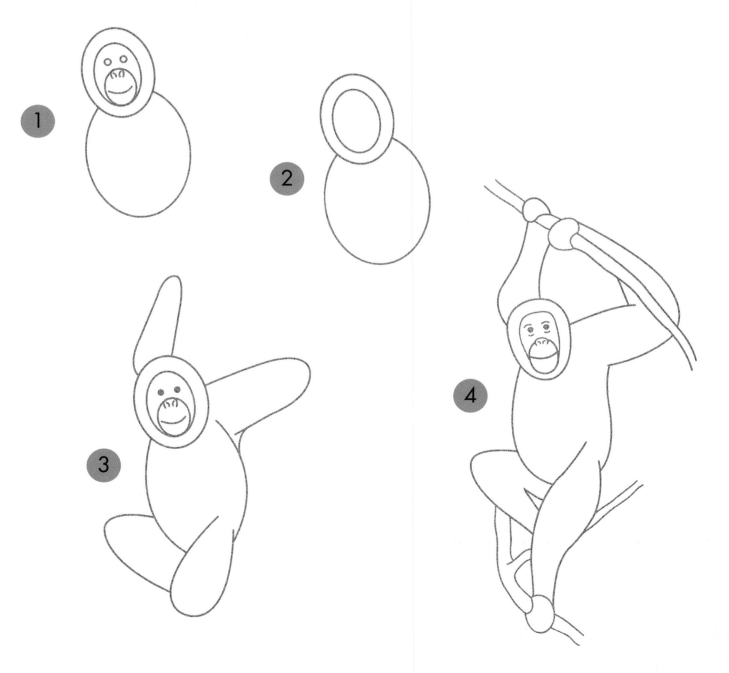

5

6

FUN FACT

Orangutans have a throat pouch that works like
a microphone, making their voices very loud.
Males, who enjoy spending time alone, have larger
pouches than females. The calls they make to keep
other orangutans from bothering them can be
heard more than a mile away!

Rabbit

No farm is complete without a few families of rabbits. Their long ears give them a keen **sense** of hearing, while their **powerful** hind legs give them the strength to make a speedy getaway—their best form of self-defense.

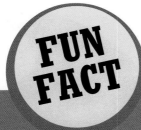

FUN FACT

Rabbits are herbivores and love to graze on grass and leafy greens. As a result, they are sometimes considered a nuisance because they may forage on young crops and can quickly eat their way through entire fields.

Cat

Farm cats are **always** busy **prowling** for small pests. Farmers appreciate them for keeping the vermin under control. In return, these frisky fellas receive a warm place to sleep and plenty of fresh milk!

Red Barn

The heart of every **farm** is its **barn**, which houses stables for the horses and provides shelter for other animals. Farmers also use the barn to store tools and equipment.

Barn Owl

This owl has a **white**, heart-shaped **face.** Its beak looks like the letter "V." This large bird likes to live in barns. That's why it's called a barn owl!

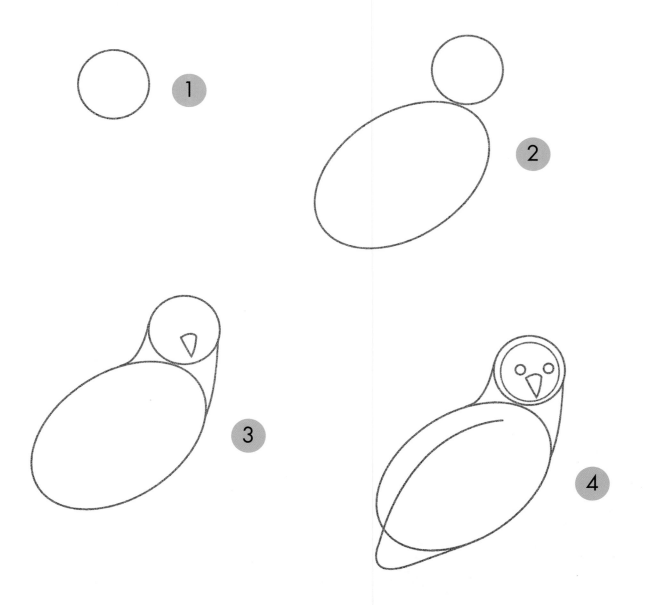

5

6

7

FUN FACT

Barn owls can locate *prey,* or animals they hunt, by sound alone. They also have excellent night vision, and their head can turn 270 degrees. Even prey hiding under plants or snow cannot escape their super senses.

Glossary

Extinct (EK-stinct) - No longer living or existing.

Endangered (en-deyn-jerd) - In danger of dying off, or becoming extinct.

Gaggle (gag-uhl) - A pack of geese when not flying.

Pesticides (pes-tuh-sahyd) - Harmful chemicals used by farmers to protect crops from pests.

Omnivore (om-nuh-vohr) - An animal that eats many different foods, including plants, fruits, and other animals.

Native (ney-tiv) – Born or from a particular place or country.

Prowl (proul) – To hunt for something, such as prey or food. When an animal is on the hunt for another animal.

Herbivore (hur-buh-vohr) - An animal that eats only plants.